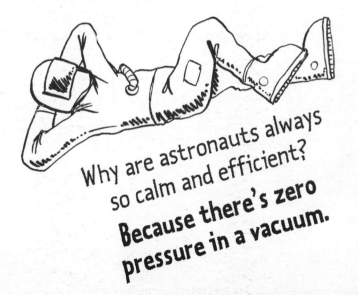

Why are astronauts always
so calm and efficient?
**Because there's zero
pressure in a vacuum.**

First published 2019 by Macmillan Children's Books
an imprint of Pan Macmillan
20 New Wharf Road, London N1 9RR
Associated companies throughout the world
www.panmacmillan.com

ISBN 978-1-5290-1517-1

1 3 5 7 9 8 6 4 2

A CIP catalogue record for this book is available from the British Library.

Compiled and illustrated by Perfect Bound Ltd
Illustrated by Dan Newman and Grace Newman

Printed and bound by CPI Group (UK) Ltd, Croydon CR0 4YY

SPACE
JOKES

MACMILLAN CHILDREN'S BOOKS

CONTENTS

ASTRONAUTS AND ROCKETS

What do astronauts
use to see at night?
Satel-lights.

How does an astronaut
get their baby to sleep?
They rocket.

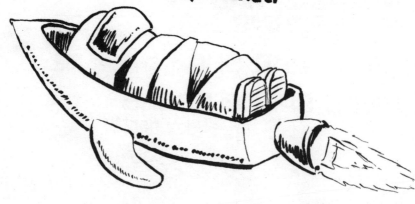

When do astronauts
retire?

**When they get
too spaced out.**

How do you arrange
an astronaut's
birthday party?

You planet.

What computer button
is an astronaut's
favourite?

The space bar.

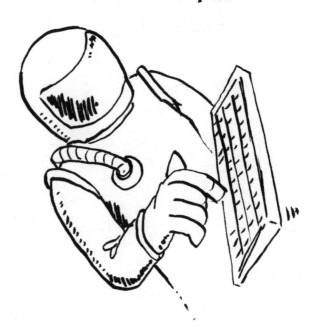

Where did the baby
astronaut want to go?
The Milky Way.

What's brown, hairy
and goes into space?
A coco-naut.

Why did the astronaut
break up with her
boyfriend?
She needed some space.

What should
a grubby
astronaut do?

**Take a meteor
shower.**

Why do some people
dislike astronauts?

**They're not very
down-to-earth.**

What happens to
naughty astronauts?
They get grounded.

I'm reading a fascinating
book about being
weightless in space.
**It's impossible
to put down.**

How do you pass
the time on a long
space journey?
**Playing astronauts
and crosses.**

Which astronaut wears
the biggest helmet?
The one with the biggest head.

Why are astronauts so successful?
They're always going up in the world.

When I grow up, I think I'll be an astronaut . . .
Well, I've got high hopes.

What happened to the astronaut who broke the laws of gravity?

He got a suspended sentence.

Astronaut: 'Are you sure we're on course to reach Mars?'

Navigator: 'Yes – why do you ask?'

Astronaut: 'Because we've just been overtaken by a number 12 bus.'

What should you do if
you see a spaceman?
Park in it, man.

What do astronauts
wear to keep warm?
Apollo-neck jumpers.

Why do astronauts make
great party guests?
**They always
have a blast.**

Did you hear about the
astronaut who fell out
of his spaceship and got
cooled to absolute zero?
He's OK now.*

*Science joke (for science nerds ...) that's zero Kelvin.

Why do astronauts wear
bulletproof vests?
**To protect themselves
from shooting stars.**

What board game do
astronauts like to play?
Moonopoly.

Why is there no doorbell at the space station?
They want to win the No-bell Prize!

Why did the astronaut go to the optician?
She had stars in her eyes.

How did the astronaut
cause an accident?

**He was getting
hot in the rocket,
so he wound down
the window.**

To save money, NASA is sending two
monkeys and an astronaut into space
next year. These are their instructions:

- Monkey #1 – pilot the rocket.

- Monkey #2 – run the
experiments.

- Astronaut – feed the monkeys.
And DON'T TOUCH ANYTHING!

Three astronauts were sent into space for a year, and they were allowed to take personal items to help pass the time. The first took a keyboard, the second took a Chinese dictionary and the third took a book of crossword puzzles.

When they returned, they were asked how they got on.

'Well, I can play the piano now,' said the first.

'And I can read Chinese now,' said the second.

'Umm . . . has anyone got a pencil?' said the third.

What do you call a
chilly spaceman?
An ice-tronaut.

And how do you
warm him up?
Give him a space heater.

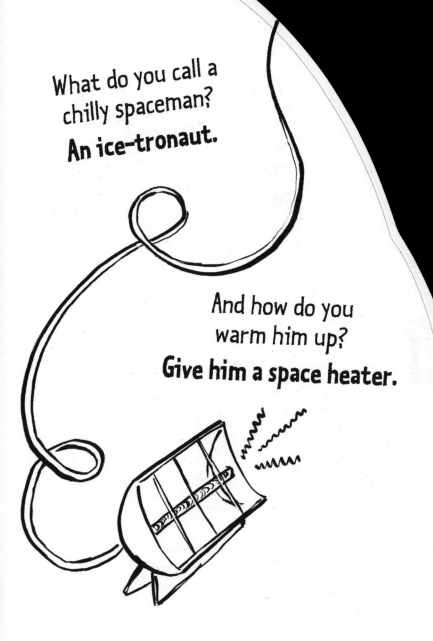

What do you call a
snake in a spacesuit?
A hiss-tronaut.

What do you call a
donkey in a spacesuit?
An ass-tronaut.

Five reasons why my nan shouldn't be an astronaut:

1 When shown the wonders of the universe she replies, 'That's nice, dear. Are there any biscuits?'

2 She insists we put on a scarf and hat before going out on a spacewalk.

3 If we meet aliens, she'll show them pictures of her cat.

4 She asks if we need to stop for petrol and a cup of tea.

5 She leaves her false teeth floating around the spaceship.

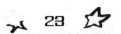

SPACE FOOD AND DRINK

Where do astronauts
keep their food?
In a launchbox.

And what does it
say on the lid?
Lift-off before eating.

Why did the hipster
astronaut burn
his tongue?

**He always ate his food
before it was cool.**

What do astronauts
like to drink?

Gravi-tea.

What's an astronaut's
favourite sweet?

Marsmallows.

What's yellow and white
and travels at 1,000
miles per hour?

An astronaut's egg sandwich.

Where's the best place
in the solar system
to go for a drink?
A Mars bar.

Where does an alien
put its teacup?
On a flying saucer.

What's the worst day to meet a hungry alien?
Chewsday.

An alien walked into a cafe and asked for a cup of coffee.

'That'll be five pounds, please,' said the barista. 'You know, we don't get a lot of aliens in here.'

'I'm not surprised,' said the alien, 'at five pounds a cup.'

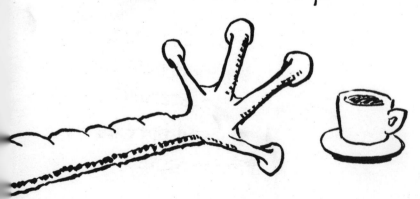

What does an alien
cook breakfast in?

**An unidentified
frying object.**

Why did the alien
throw some ham on
to the asteroid?

**He wanted it to be
a little meteor.**

Alien kid: 'Mum, when will dinner be ready? I'm starving!'

Alien mum: 'Stop moaning! I've only got three pairs of hands.'

What do aliens have for breakfast?
E. T. bix.

What do aliens spread
on their toast?
Marsmalade.

Why won't aliens
eat clowns?
**Because they
taste funny.**

I met an alien who eats watches, but it takes ages for him to finish each one.

It's very time-consuming.

What do you say to an alien with rhubarb growing out of its head?

You should put some cream on that.

That alien just threw
milk, cheese and
yoghurt all over me.
How dairy!

How do you know if an alien
has been in your fridge?
**There are footprints
in the butter.**

Did you hear about
the alien who ate
an entire planet?

**I know, it's pretty
hard to swallow.**

'My uncle was abducted by
aliens last week while he was
in the garden picking peas.'
 'How terrible! What did
your auntie do?'
 'She had to use frozen
peas instead.'

Why do aliens never get hungry in space? **Because they always know where to find a Milky Way, a Mars and a Galaxy.**

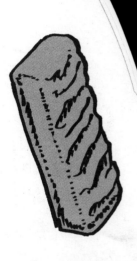

I dream that, somewhere out there, there's a planet with a fizzy orange ocean. **But it's just a Fanta-sea.**

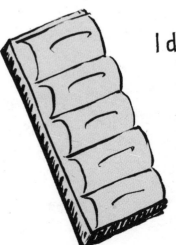

The French built
a satellite out of
different cheeses, but
it exploded in orbit.
**All that was left
was de-brie.**

What is an astronaut's
favourite meal?
**Stew, because it's
meaty-all-right.**

Why don't astronauts get hungry after being blasted into space?
Because they've just had a big launch.

What do hungry aliens travel in?
A Chew-F-O.

What cheese goes best on a space pizza? **Mars-arella.**

Did you hear about the astronaut who stepped in some chewing gum?
He was stuck in Orbit.

Why are aliens messy tea-drinkers?
With flying saucers, it's hard not to spill.

What is a dalek's
favourite drink?
Exterminade!

What do small
robots have
as a snack?
Micro-chips.

What does a Time
Lord like to eat
with his pizza?
Dalek bread.

Did you hear about the
alien who only ate sofas?

**It had a really
suite tooth.**

PLANETS AND SPACE OBJECTS

What's the opposite of a meteorite?

A meteo-wrong.

How does the solar system keep its trousers on?

With an asteroid belt.

Where do planets go to study?
Universe-ity.

Have you seen the fantastic TV series about black holes?
You'll definitely get sucked in.

How does Earth tease
the other planets?
'You guys have no life.'

What did one shooting
star say to the other?
Pleased to meteor!

Why is Saturn
called Saturn?
It has a nice ring to it.

Why did Mickey Mouse
go to outer space?
To find Pluto.

What did Neptune
say to Saturn?
**Give me a ring
sometime.**

What kind of songs
do planets sing?
Nep-tunes.

What kind of
poetry can you find
in outer space?
Uni-verse.

How do we know
Mars is bald?

**Because it ain't
got no 'air.**

Scientists have sent
a probe to the centre
of Jupiter ...
**and discovered it
is the letter 'i'.**

How many astronomers
does it take to change
a light bulb?
**Nobody knows –
they're perfectly
happy in the dark.**

What's the most dangerous object in space?

A shooting star.

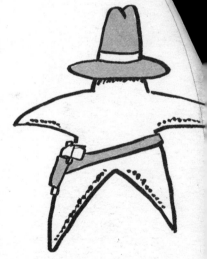

How do we know Saturn is rich?

Because it wears all those rings!

Why doesn't the Dog
Star laugh at jokes?
Because it's too Sirius.

Here on Earth my cat
weighs 8kg, but on Mars he
would weigh only 3kg.
**So he's not fat – he's just
on the wrong planet.**

What kind of stars
wear dark glasses?
Movie stars.

The density of Saturn is so low that
it would actually float in a bath. You
shouldn't try this, however, as it's bound
to leave a **massive** ring round the tub.

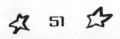

Personally, I don't think there's intelligent life on other planets.

Why should other planets be any different from this one?

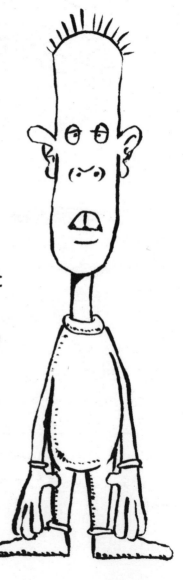

Jupiter came down to Earth one day and helped two criminals organize a bank robbery. They both got caught and, after the judge sentenced the two earthlings to fifteen years behind bars, Jupiter was a bit shocked to get arrested and handed a ten-year stretch himself.

'But, Your Honour, I didn't even take part in the robbery!' said Jupiter.

'Yes,' replied the judge. 'But you did help them planet!"

What do planets read?
Comet books.

What is the largest
ocean in space?
The Galax-sea.

What's a black hole?
What you find in old black socks.

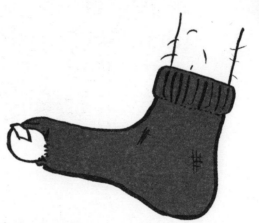

I think Earth is absolutely brilliant.
All it has to do is turn round and it just makes my day.

All the jokes about gravity are really old ...

But I still fall for them every time.

A group that was certain the Earth is flat decided to walk to the edge to prove it.

It took a while, but in the end they came round.

ALIENS

Should you be worried
about an alien with
no left arm or leg?

**No, because
he's all right.**

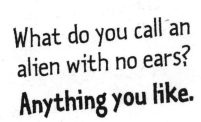

What do you call an
alien with no ears?

Anything you like.

What did the alien
say to the cat?
Take me to your litter.

What should you do if
you see a green alien?
Wait until it's ripe.

What do you get if
you cross a kangaroo
with an alien?

A Mars-upial.

What should you
do if you see
a blue alien?

**Try to cheer
it up.**

What should you
do if you see a
one-legged alien?
Tell them to hop it.

What should you
do if you see an
angry alien?
**Give it some
space.**

What do you call an
alien magician?

A flying saucer-er.

What do you call an alien
that lives in a swamp?

A marsh-in.

How does an alien
count to seventeen?
**On its fingers,
of course!**

What do you call an
alien made of paper?
Russell.

Why should you never
be nasty to an alien?
**You might hurt
its feelers.**

What do you call
an alien with
three eyes?
An aliiien.

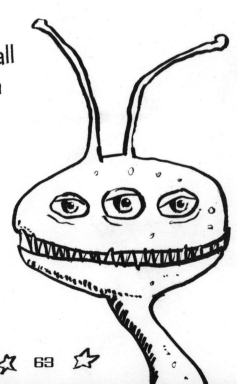

What did the alien say
to the petrol pump?

**Take your finger out
of your ear when
I'm talking to you!**

How do you know when
there's an alien hiding
in your bathroom?

**You can't close the
shower curtain.**

What do you call a sick
extra-terrestrial?

An ailin' alien.

Can aliens jump higher
than a lamp post?

**Of course – lamp
posts can't jump.**

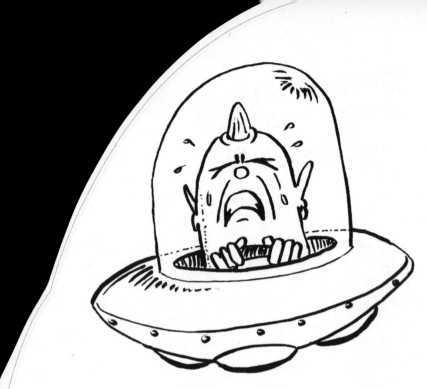

Where will you find
a sad alien?

In a crying saucer.

Why is an annoying
alien like a bogey?

**Because it's small,
green and gets
up your nose.**

What do you say to an alien with three heads?

Hello, hello, hello.

What's green and invisible?

No aliens.

A woman at a petrol station was surprised to see a spaceship pull in. An alien got out and started to fill it up with petrol.

'Excuse me,' said the woman. 'Those letters on your spaceship, UFO ... does that stand for Unidentified Flying Object?'

'No,' replied the alien, 'it stands for Unleaded Fuel Only.'

What do you find stuck
between the toes
of giant aliens?
Slow humans.

What should an alien
wear to a wedding?
A spacesuit.

What do you call a spaceship
with no air conditioning?

A frying saucer.

What did the alien say
to the metric system?
Take me to your litre.

Knock knock!
Who's there?
An alien!
An alien who?
Wait, how many aliens do you know?

How do you stop invading aliens from charging?
Take away their credit cards.

What do you
call an alien in
Trafalgar Square?
Lost.

What should
you do if you
find a massive
alien asleep
in your bed?

**Sleep on
the sofa.**

Alien: 'So where are you from?'

Astronaut: 'Earth.'

Alien: 'Really? What part?'

Astronaut: 'All of me.'

Invisible aliens are useless at lying.

You can see right through them.

Which singer do
aliens listen to?
Bruno Mars.

Why don't we
spot aliens
hiding in trees?
**Because
they're really
good at it.**

Why is an alien
like a banana?
**They're both yellow,
except for the alien.**

What currency
do aliens use?
Star-bucks.

What do you call an
overweight alien?

An extra-cholesterol.

Why haven't aliens
visited Earth yet?

**They read the reviews for
our solar system and were
put off – only one star.**

What's the difference between an alien and a loaf of bread?

Don't know? Well, I'm not sending you to the shops, then.

How do you keep an alien busy for three hours?

Give them a piece of paper with 'Please Turn Over' written on both sides.

I wasn't sure if I wanted the aliens to swap my brain . . . **Until they changed my mind.**

An alien landed on Earth near a supermarket. It went in and stared at a carton of orange juice for three hours . . . because it said 'concentrate'.

Aliens have given us a Universal Remote Control.
This changes everything.

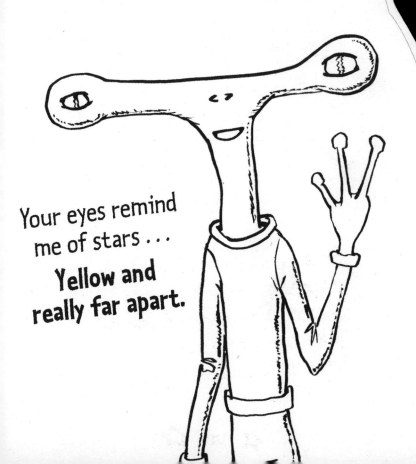

Your eyes remind me of stars . . .
Yellow and really far apart.

EXTRA-TERRESTRIAL TU

What's brown, smelly and travels through time?
Doctor Poo.

Where does Doctor Who buy his cheese?
At a dalek-atessen.

'What do we want?'
'Time-travel jokes!'
When do we want them?'
'It doesn't matter!'

What's it called when the Doctor goes back in time and sees himself?

A time-travel pair-o'-docs.

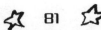

I've got a dalek
egg timer.
**After three minutes it
says, 'Eggs – terminate.'**

What do you call a
time-travelling cow?
Doctor Moo.

Why do daleks eat
so much fruit?

**Because an apple a day
keeps the Doctor away.**

Waiter: 'Wait, I'm confused.'
The Doctor: 'Coffee, please.'
Waiter: 'What can I get you?'
A Time Lord walks into a cafe . . .

The Doctor has
won awards for his
amazing herbs.
He's a Thyme Lord.

Why is Doctor
Who so useful
to know?

**He always tries
his Tardis
to help.**

What time is it
when a dalek runs
over your foot?
Time to call a Doctor.

How do you negotiate
with a cyberman?
**From a very long
way away.**

What's the
opposite of K9?
Kit10.

Who's the scariest
Time Lord?
Doctor BOO!

Knock knock!
Who's there?
Art.
Art who?
R2-D2.

How did Darth Vader know
what Luke Skywalker got
him for Christmas?

He felt his presents.

What do you call an invisible robot?
C-through-PO.

Why didn't the boy eat his Wookie steak?
It was a bit Chewie.

Darth has a little
sister who's going
up in the world.
She's called Ellie Vader.

Why did R2-D2 and
C-3PO go on holiday?
**To recharge their
batteries.**

What do you call
Chewbacca with little
bits of chocolate
stuck in his fur?

**A chocolate chip
Wookie.**

What does a Jedi use
to open PDF files?

Adobe-Wan Kenobi.

What did Obi-Wan say
to Luke Skywalker
at dinner time?
'Use the forks, Luke.'

What's a Jedi's
favourite toy?
A yo-Yoda.

What do you call a
pirate droid?
Arrr-2-D2.

What is Jabba the
Hutt's middle name?
The.

BIG SWEATY BULLY LICENCE

surname
HUTT

first names
JABBA, THE

address
PALACE, TATOOINE

Why did the angry
Jedi cross the road?
To get to the dark side.

What did the Emperor
say to Darth Vader?
Merry Sithmas.

Who serves the food in the
Death Star cafeteria?
Darth Waiter.

How do you know Yoda
is a good gardener?
He's got a green thumb.

How do you get a
one-armed Klingon
out of a tree?
Wave at him.

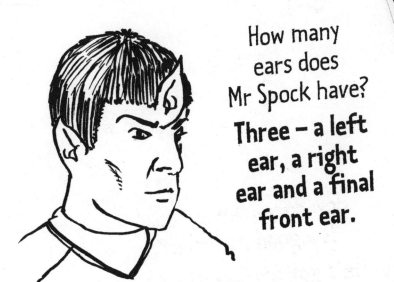

How many
ears does
Mr Spock have?
**Three – a left
ear, a right
ear and a final
front ear.**

Why did the chicken
cross the galaxy?
**To boldly go where
no chicken had
gone before.**

And how did she
get there?
**On the *Starship
Henterprise*.**

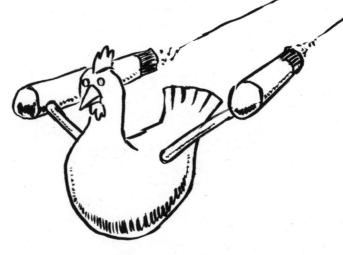

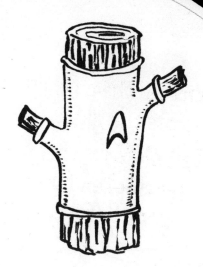

I went to a Star Trek
fancy dress party
dressed as a tree.

I was the captain's log.

How does a Romulan
frog hide?

**It uses a croaking
device.**

What does a short-sighted
Vulcan wear?

Spocktacles.

How many Klingons does it
take to change a lightbulb?

**None! Klingons do not fear
darkness! Dishonour on
the lightbulb for failing!**

Why couldn't the
Enterprise travel
faster than light?
Its engines got warped.

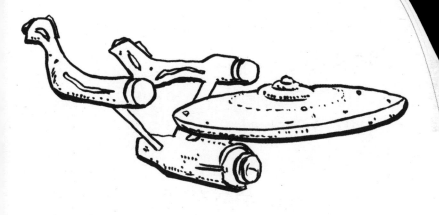

If Spock has pointy ears,
what does Scotty have?
Engineers.

ROCKETS AND SPACESHIPS

Where should you park a spaceship?
At a parking meteor.

Did you hear about
the rocket that
lost its job?
It got fired.

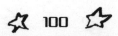

What do you get when you whack your foot on a rocket?

Missile-toe.

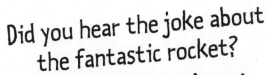

Did you hear the joke about the fantastic rocket?

You'll love it – it's out of this world. But it'll probably go over your head.

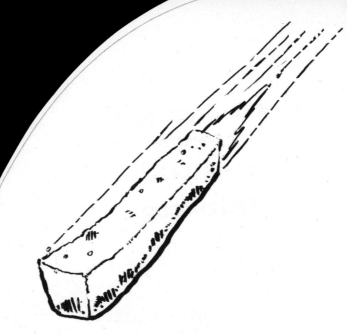

What's fast, loud
and crunchy?
A rocket chip.

Mum didn't believe
there was a rocket
made of spaghetti.
**You should have seen
her face when it flew
straight pasta.**

Where are reasonably
acceptable
rockets made?
In a satis-factory.

What should you do if
you crash a rocket?
Apollo-gise.

What vegetable do
you not want on
a rocket trip?
A leek.

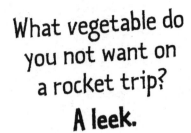

I tried to start
a business
selling broken
rocket parts.
**It didn't
take off.**

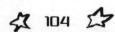

I got my friend a
massive rocket for
fireworks night.

**He is quite literally
over the moon about it.**

I launched my own
clothing line last week.

**That'll teach me to set off a
rocket next to the washing.**

Why was Mission
Control deserted?
**Everyone was out
to launch.**

I watched a show about
how rockets are built.
It was rivet-ing.

NASA has made a
rocket out of the same
material as whiteboards.
It's re-markable.

Why did the cow get
on a spaceship?
**To get to the
moooooooon.**

How do lambs get
to the moon?

In a spacesheep.

How do you know
if there's an alien
in your house?

**There's a spaceship
parked in your garden.**

Knock knock!
Who's there?
Jupiter.
Jupiter who?
**Jupiter spaceship
on my lawn?**

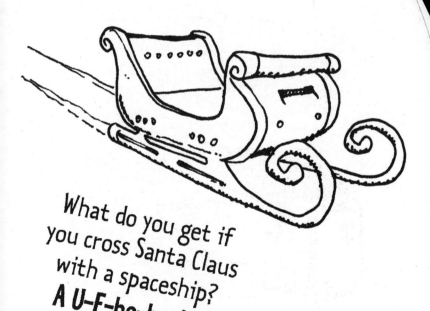

What do you get if
you cross Santa Claus
with a spaceship?
A U-F-ho-ho-ho.

Who are the slowest
creatures in space?
Snailiens.

How did the astronaut
find out his rocket had
caught the Miley virus?
It stopped twerking.

Why couldn't the rocket
land on the moon?
It was full.

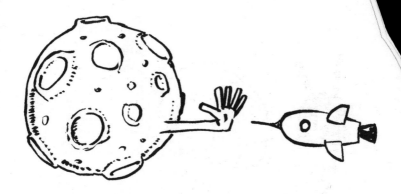

I want to tell you this
great joke about how
I built a rocket . . .
**but I can't – I'm still
working on it.**

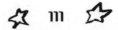

MOON AND SUN

Why are restaurants on the moon so unpopular? **They have no atmosphere.**

What's the best day to launch a rocket? **Moonday.**

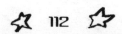

When is the moon
not hungry?
When it's full.

Which is further away,
Spain or the moon?
Spain, obviously.
Really? Why do you think that?
**Because I can see the
moon from here!**

Which is heavier – the Earth, Mars or the sun?

The Earth, because Mars is a chocolate bar and the _Sun_ is a newspaper.

How does a barber cut the moon's hair?

'E clipse it.

How many sausages
would it take to reach all
the way to the moon?
**Just one . . . if it's
big enough.**

Why did the sun
go to school?
To get brighter.

And where did it
go after school?
Mooniversity.

How clever is the sun?
**Well, it's got over
5,000 degrees.**

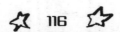

What's a light year?
The same as a regular year, but with fewer calories.

What holds
the moon up?
Moon beams.

What's round,
bright and silly?
A fool moon.

I was up all night
wondering where the
sun had gone . . .
Then it dawned on me.

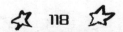

Three people were showing off about their countries.

'We were the first country in space,' said the first.

'So what,' said the second. 'We were the first country to land on the moon.'

'That's nothing,' said the third. 'We're going to land on the sun.'

'How are you going to do that?' asked the other two.

'It's easy. We'll go at night, of course!'

What do moon people do
after they get married?

**They go on a
honeyearth.**

Two people were pointing in the sky
and arguing. 'That's the moon up
there, I tell you!' shouted the first.
  'No, it's the sun, definitely!' said
the second. They couldn't agree, so
they asked a passer-by.
  'I don't know,' he said. 'I've only
lived here a week.'

What was the first
animal in space?
**The cow that jumped
over the moon.**

What do you call an
insect on the moon?
A luna-tick.

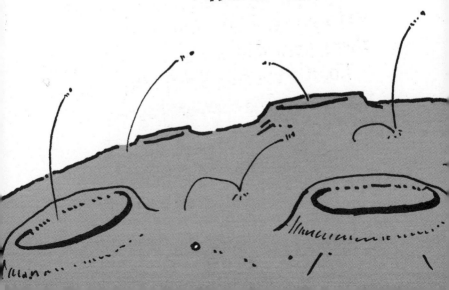

Which is heavier,
a full moon or
a half moon?

**A half moon,
because a full
moon is lighter.**

Living on Earth might
be expensive . . .

**but at least we get
a free trip round
the sun every year.**

When is the moon short
of American money?

**When it's down to
its last quarter.**

What did the therapist
say to the moon?

**It's just a phase you're
going through.**

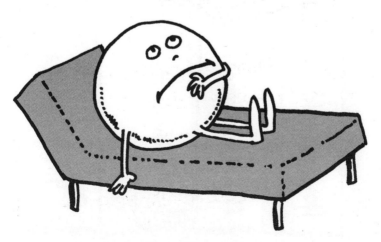

SILLY SPACE BOOKS

How to Build a Robot by Anne Droid

The Scary Extra-terrestrial by Hugh Jalien

My Favourite Planet by V. Nuss

How We Defeated the Aliens by Vic Tree

Flying Space Rocks by S. Steroid

Dealing with Smelly Aliens by Stan Wellback

They Came Without Warning by Oliver Sudden

Upgrade your Computer by Meg Abights

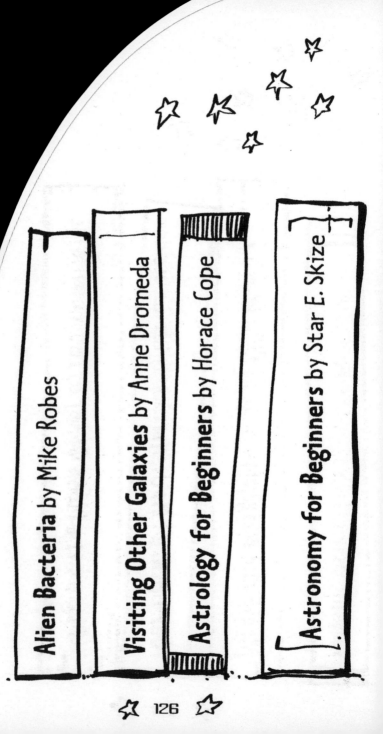

Alien Bacteria by Mike Robes

Visiting Other Galaxies by Anne Dromeda

Astrology for Beginners by Horace Cope

Astronomy for Beginners by Star E. Skize

Russian Space Travel by Cosmo Knott

Artificial Weightlessness by Andy Gravity

Complicated Mathematics by Cal Q. Luss

Where's the Moon Gone? by Lou Narey-Klips